Aging Gracefully

Aging Gracefully

The Keys to Holier, Happier Golden Years

J. Daniel Dymski

Foreword by
Archbishop Rembert G. Weakland, OSB

ACTA

ASSISTING CHRISTIANS TO ACT

PUBLICATIONS

Aging Gracefully
The Keys to Holier, Happier Golden Years
by J. Daniel Dymski
Foreword by Archbishop Rembert G. Weakland, OSB

Edited by Gregory F. Augustine Pierce
Cover design by Tom A. Wright
Typesetting by Desktop Edit Shop, Inc.

Published by: ACTA Publications
                 Assisting Christians To Act
                 4848 N. Clark Street
                 Chicago, IL 60640-4711
                 773-271-1030

Library of Congress Catalog Number: 2002104338
ISBN: 0-87946-232-9
Printed in the United States of America
Printing: 10 9 8 7 6 5 4 3 2 1
Year: 08 07 06 05 04 03 02

Contents

This book is dedicated to all the wonderful older adults with whom I have had the privilege of ministering over the years. By their wisdom and example they have taught me about holiness and happiness in the golden years of life.

Foreword

by Archbishop Rembert G. Weakland, OSB

Everywhere around the world these days—with but few very sad exceptions—people are living longer. Most of us can foresee the day when the advanced age now reached by some exceptional oldsters will become commonplace. Our scientific advances make it possible to live much longer than our predecessors ever dreamed. But what about the quality of this extended life? Are people necessarily happier because they are living longer? In itself, one could say that longevity is neither good nor bad and that so much depends on what each one of us will make of it. Most of us do not want to live longer just for the sake of breaking some kind of record.

If people are now able to live longer because of the advances of medicine, then the quality of their extended lives should make such longevity worthwhile. But so much is up to the individual and the attitudes that the individual has toward life and especially toward life in these older years. The question is not just about a long life but a meaningful and fruitful one.

First of all, living longer cannot be an evasion of our own mortality. Whatever is human, whatever is made up of flesh and bones, whatever is created cannot of itself endure forever. Facing our own mortality is still very necessary as we make the older years more fruitful. Death and afterlife must still be prepared for, even if the time allotted us is greater than we may have imagined in our youth.

But facing up to our mortality means a strong faith in God and more reflection on God's plan for each of us in our older years. If we live longer, then our faith should be strong in giving meaning to those years. All the motives we had for existence in our younger years—to live for others, to cultivate our talents and gifts for the betterment of this world, to share with all those dear to us—remain, even if perhaps at times they have to be re-burnished. All these motives for active living are still valid, even if the emphasis shifts. In addition, however, we are given more time to reflect on the future God has planned for us that until now has been seen but in a distance. Living longer, thus, can give more time for preparing for that ultimate union with God.

One could sum up all of these truths by saying that longer years are not necessarily better years unless we decide to make them so. Father Dan Dymski tells us how to do just that. He works on our attitudes because he knows that our attitudes are what make the difference. He has arranged these attitudes around what he calls the "keys to holier, happier golden years." More than anything else, he helps us make these added years positive ones— physically, mentally and spiritually. He shows us how to let the faith dimension of our lives take over so that we see these years as gift and not burden.

When life is seen as a journey, the arrival at our destination should be the happiest part of the trip. As we approach our goal, we should become more and more excited about arriving there. Our expectation levels should grow stronger. All the negatives of the trip should fade away at the thought of finally reaching our goal. In our case, as people of faith, that goal is ultimate union with God and with all of those who went before us whose memory we hold so dear in our hearts.

This book will help all of us keep this ultimate goal in mind and serve us well in preparing for it. It is practical and clear, faith directed but full of human wisdom. It is directed toward this life but does not neglect the hereafter. It unifies the approaches we must have toward this life and toward the next so that there is a continuum between them.

Blessings on all those who heed the words of Father Dymski.

Introduction

Gray hair is a crown of glory; it is gained in a righteous life.

Proverbs 16:31

We have no choice about growing old, but the choice of how we spend our aging years is entirely our own. For some of us, old age can be a pleasant and enjoyable stage of life—one even anticipated with eagerness. There is no inherent reason why our closing years should not be as exhilarating, stimulating, and fruitful as our opening ones. If we are to know serenity and joy in our old age, however, we must find the keys to maintaining a positive and cheerful outlook.

Some people have learned to tap sources of strength that enable them to reach even greater heights of their potential as they age. They have seen beyond their limitations to the opportunities, possibilities and compensations that senior status can bring. As we look throughout history, we can find role models who had a mind-set that helped them get the best out of aging. Think of Dorothy Day, Pope John Paul II, Jimmy and Rosalyn Carter, Mother Teresa and so many others. There is a great potential, largely untapped, in the accumulated knowledge, experience and perseverance of older adults. They are the ones who greatly enrich our world when they release and utilize their hidden resources.

Such people refuse to concede defeat to Father Time. Their very resilience is a great encouragement to those of us who are determined to discover their secret. In the parable of the workers in the vineyard, we read that the landowner went out "about five o'clock" and said to a group of workers, "You also go into the vineyard" (Matthew 20:7). As we reach the "late afternoon" of our lives, God—our landowner, if you will—challenges and encourages us to keep working and growing, right to the very end. For it is God's plan that old age should be the crowning glory of a person's lifetime.

If we are blessed with long years, and realize our pilgrimage on this earth is coming to the sunset, old age can be a golden opportunity for intellectual growth, spiritual growth and deep happiness. Even though there are limitations with older age, it can still be a time of productivity and vitality that opens up new horizons of joyous possibilities and a great deal of happiness.

The most important thing needed is to age gracefully. We know that with advancing years there is often wisdom. This wisdom has been hammered out, often painfully, on the anvil of real life experiences. As we grow older, we have the opportunity and privilege of sharing this wisdom with others. This is a great potential, like a sleeping giant, which is largely untapped in our society. This potential can be made available when more attention is given to realizing and utilizing the hidden talents and resources of older adults.

This book is meant to provide you, the reader, with spiritual nourishment and growth in your "golden years." Each of the twelve "keys" addresses a single issue in the process of aging with grace.

Each key begins with a passage from Sacred Scripture meant to illustrate the key's primary point. This is followed by some observations grouped around a single concept that is vital to successfully turning that key. My style is to suggest rather than direct, and I am not afraid to repeat important points. I utilize aphorisms, which are concise statements of a truth that are intended for reflection and slow assimilation. These are followed by questions for individual reflection or group discussion to help more fully explore the meaning of the key. Finally, there are suggested actions to help individuals or a group apply the concepts of the key to daily life.

So I invite you to unlock the twelve keys to holier, joy-filled aging years. God be with you on your journey.

The First Key
Adopt a Positive Attitude

*Let your gentleness be known to everyone.
The LORD is near. Do not worry about
anything, but in everything by prayer and
supplication with thanksgiving let your
requests be made known to God. And the
peace of God, which surpasses all
understanding, will guard your hearts and
your minds in Christ Jesus.*

Philippians 4:5-7

On Attitude

O⎯ Old age is not about arteries but attitude.

O⎯ It is in our attitude that we discover strength
or weakness, hope or fear, determination or
frustration.

O⎯ There is very little in our lives over which we
have full control. However, in one area of our

17

lives, we do have much control. That area is our attitude.

O━ The attitude we choose to express teaches those around us what to expect from us and from one another.

O━ If we have a positive attitude we can shine like beacons: "You are the light of the world.... Let your light shine before others, so that they may see your good works and give glory to your Father in heaven" (Matthew 5:14-16).

O━ Only we can determine whether our attitude will be positive or not. The choice rests with us.

O━ We need to look at our attitude toward aging and realize that it is possible to change or deepen our perception of growing older.

O━ Being positive will change our life.

O━ When we stop thinking only of our problems, we will rediscover a great, loving world around us.

On Turning Our Life Over to God

- ⚷ "Let go and let God," they say in Alcoholics Anonymous.

- ⚷ Focusing our attention on matters that disturb us keeps us disturbed.

- ⚷ When we become obsessed with problems, there is no room for solutions.

- ⚷ We need to search for the good that may be lost in an unsettled situation.

- ⚷ We need to let go of problems and move ahead, not allow ourselves to be trapped by circumstances beyond our control.

- ⚷ When we turn into ourselves, we may sense how often we are inclined to look only at the unpleasant side of things.

- ⚷ In doing so, we fail to celebrate the many opportunities aging grants us to become more grateful.

- ⚷ When we get to heaven, God will not ask us our age but how well we have lived, what our priorities were in life, and if we have been grateful servants.

On Being Happy

O— We carry within ourselves the ability to make our final years and days happy.

O— We can be grateful for our blessings or resentful that we have only what we have.

O— The power to be happy is at our fingertips.

O— If we greet the day with a smile, we will discover that life holds great promise and new areas of joyous experiences will open to us.

O— If we do not fight old age, old age will be the best age of all.

O— Aging is not a reason for despair but a basis for hope. It is not a slow decaying but a gradual maturing, not a fate to be undergone but an opportunity to be embraced.

O— In our Western World, the fear of becoming old is determined primarily by the fear of not being able to live up to the expectations of an environment in which we are what we can produce, achieve, have and keep.

O— We tend to travel in a world of our own making. We can close ourselves off from the possibilities of new life styles that might challenge us to take risks and to change.

⊙━ As we age, we are challenged to believe in the value of just being alive, to believe there is something precious and holy in waking up each morning to a new day.

⊙━ We can offer love to our fellow travelers in life or we can harbor envy toward them.

⊙━ Stepping back and getting a different perspective on a situation will help us realize that solutions are always within our grasp. Often, sharing with others helps us achieve this perspective.

⊙━ To compare our present life with that of others or with our former lifestyle can make us unhappy and maybe even depressed. No one should live a life of fantasy based on the past. We need to live in the present-day conditions that are God's will for us now.

On Being Grateful

⊙━ To grow spiritually in our later years is only possible when we live in real gratitude. Only the thankful older adult will see God in a sunny day, in a flower along the sidewalk, in the pleasant smile of a friend or loved one.

- Gratefulness is the secret of gracious aging. To spend the closing years of our life without thanks is to dwell in desperation of the good things that come our way.

- While growing in gratitude, we need to explore new avenues of interest, purpose and aspiration.

- The art of saying thank you to God is the best prevention of despondency or discouragement. The fruits of gratefulness bring a whole new life to the soul.

- We need to thank God on our tough days as well as our easy ones.

- We should try to keep our minds and hearts open while abiding in prayerful expectation.

- If we prod ourselves to accept God's spiritual help, we will discover a new light that will help us find something for which we can be thankful.

- If we look carefully at the world around us, we can see that the list of things for which we can give thanks is literally endless.

- When we look for these opportunities, we will feel the surge of a new sense of joy and of being alive.

○━ A grateful disposition does not come to us immediately, as if by magic. Gratefulness can be formed in us only gradually, step by step.

○━ God will not force gratefulness upon us.

Questions for Reflection or Discussion

1. How do you feel about yourself at your present age?

2. In what ways has your spiritual life changed as you have grown older?

3. Give an example of how aging has affected your dealings with others in a positive way. Now give an example of how it has negatively affected your dealings with others.

4. What positive aspects of aging do you give thanks for?

5. To what extent have you turned your life over to God? What has been the result?

Suggestions for Action

■ *Make a list of at least five God-given talents you have and should be utilizing in your daily life.*

■ *Spend at least ten minutes each day in prayerful meditation requesting the guidance and inspiration of the Holy Spirit on specific ways you could make your life more meaningful for yourself and others. During the day, try to implement one of these changes.*

The Second Key
Trust in God

Therefore I tell you, do not worry about your life, what you will eat or drink, or about your body, what you will wear. Is not life more than food and the body more than clothing? Look at the birds of the air; they neither sown or reap nor gather into barns, and yet your heavenly Father feeds them. Are you not of more value than they? And can any of you by worrying add a single hour to your span of life? And why do you worry about clothing? Consider the lilies of the field, how they grow; they neither toil nor spin, yet I tell you, even Solomon in all his glory was not clothed like one of these. But if God so clothes the grass of the field, which is alive today and tomorrow is thrown into the oven, will he not much more clothe you—you of little faith? Therefore do not worry, saying, "What will we eat" or "What will we drink?" or "What will we wear?"

Matthew 6:25-31

On Putting Aside Worries

O—π As we adults grow older, we often experience the poverty of our physical and spiritual weaknesses. So much of what we did when we were younger is no longer possible.

O—π What makes our pain and suffering bearable is knowing that we are deeply loved by God.

O—π Trust in God allows us to put aside our worries, to forgive our sisters and brothers, to focus on the present moment, to give of ourselves to others, and to seek love everywhere.

O—π If we focus only on our physical frailties as we grow older, we can easily find ourselves falling into despair or even a state of despondency. Faith is what enables us to experience happiness, despite our troubles.

O—π We may need to examine ourselves to see if we are using our busyness to hide our pain or avoid the pain of the future.

O—π Because of faith, we can live with the assurance that God's love is always there, no matter what human adversity may befall us.

O—π Faith enhances our power to love and be loved.

○—ㅠ People often talk about a crisis in their life, but we have all heard others say, "It was my faith that pulled me through."

○—ㅠ Faith is the gift God gives to strengthen us to accept God's will instead of trying to force God to do things according to our will.

On Prayer and Meditation

○—ㅠ We need to seek conscious contact with God through prayer and meditation.

○—ㅠ God wants us, his aging children, to have abiding faith in the significance and purpose of our lives.

○—ㅠ We read in Psalm 116:1-2: "I love the LORD, because he has heard my voice and my supplications. Because he inclined his ear to me, therefore I will call on him as long as I live."

○—ㅠ Some of us seem to have a hard time praying. We do not seem to have enough time to pray. Even if we do have a quiet free period, our prayers seem to sometimes fall short of what we wish them to be and are often filled with distractions.

- For interior or private prayer there is a need for silence in the midst of noise, a need for peace amid today's outbursts of violence throughout the world, a need to feel the warmth of God's love when everything is being rationalized or computerized, and a need for slowness to compensate for the current infatuation with speed.

- The bottom line is that we need an interior life to prepare ourselves for what lies ahead.

On a Spiritual Retirement Plan

- In most cases, as we grow older we carefully prepare a financial retirement plan. The earlier we begin, the better. We also need to prepare a spiritual retirement plan.

- No matter what our age, we need to take steps to enrich our spiritual life by deepening our current life of faith and freely sharing with others what we have learned from our experiences of God.

- Like our human relationships, our faith relationship with God needs time, attention, perseverance and love if it is to develop and grow.

- When our spiritual or interior life is strong, our attitude toward others is gentle.

- When our spiritual life is nourished, our hearts and feelings will be open to appreciating and understanding others' joys and sorrows.

- Our spiritual teachers constantly remind us that when we have a gentle, healthy and strong spiritual life, we are part of the process of healing the world, offering hope to all who suffer and yearn for justice, solace and encouragement.

On Patience and Perseverance

- Spiritual gratification is not always immediate. We cannot rush God's plans for us.

- *Patience* and *perseverance* are words that we need to put back into our vocabulary.

- Spiritual wisdom requires us to question the voices that are guiding our lives. If we entrust ourselves to the Holy Spirit, we will be better able to judge why we believe, think and act as we do.

○━ As we grow older, we have the potential for immense creativity. We have a chance to re-discover ourselves and be energized to reach a fuller meaning of life.

○━ As we grow closer to full maturity, we may see things on a wider scale. Older adults are challenged not merely to look ahead to the end of life's journey but to take time, here and now, to look back on all we have learned.

○━ Yet spiritual growth also demands that we let go of the past so we can grow beyond it, even though we know that such letting go and trusting can be a painful process.

○━ As we grow older, we sometimes give up some comforting security. We can no longer always follow our familiar ways, and our world may become narrow, confining and limited.

○━ As we age, we can enter into a fuller, deeper experience of life. We learn that the pain of letting go of the past and the joy of rising in the newness of life will always be there.

○━ As we grow older, we have a tendency to look for a life of simplicity, yet we also can begin to think of new ideas in fresh ways.

On Journeying with Jesus

⚬⇥ It is possible to experience a real breakdown of our trust in God as we grow older. We can be tempted to doubt or find it hard to believe that God truly loves us.

⚬⇥ We need to journey with Jesus, to relive his suffering, death and resurrection.

⚬⇥ On the cross, Jesus affirmed that God's grace is present even in the midst of the worst. God builds his kingdom in a non-worldly way—not through strength but through weakness.

⚬⇥ "For God so loved the world that he gave his only Son, so that everyone who believes in him may not perish but may have eternal life. Indeed, God did not send his Son into the world to condemn the world, but in order that the world might be saved through him" (John 3:16-17).

⚬⇥ If we find it hard to take up our own crosses each day, the sight of the crucifix will remind us that the sinless Jesus, who carried his cross to Calvary and died on it, needs the crosses of all of us to be willingly borne if his death is to be effective for the salvation of humanity.

⊙── The apostle Paul said it this way: "I am now rejoicing in my sufferings for your sake, and in my flesh I am completing what is lacking in Christ's afflictions for the sake of his body, that is, the church" (Colossians 1:24).

⊙── Faith does not make the deprivations and debilities of aging easy, but it can make suffering meaningful.

Questions for Reflection or Discussion

1. How has aging contributed to your ability to deepen your trust in God? Give an example of how you have been able to "put aside" some of your worries.

2. Imagine how "giving up the past" can help you gain a better future.

3. Give an example of ways your trust in God has changed over the last decade.

4. How might you better practice patience and perseverance in you prayer?

5. Has your faith ever pulled you through a personal crisis? What happened?

Suggestions for Action

■ *Pick up a Bible and open it anywhere at random. Flip through and read until you find a passage that describes someone who put his or her faith in God. (It shouldn't be difficult, for that is what the entire Bible is about!) Then reflect on how you can better put your own trust in God and how your life might change if you did.*

■ *Begin your own "spiritual retirement plan." Write down how you are going to insure that you work on your interior life on a regular basis. Be specific!*

The Third Key
Appreciate the Present Moment

*For it is as if a man, going on a journey,
summoned his slaves and entrusted his property
to them; to one he gave five talents, to another
two, to another one, to each according to his
ability. Then he went away. The one who had
received the five talents went off at once and
traded with them, and made five more talents.
In the same way, the one who had the two
talents made two more talents. But the one who
had received the one talent went off and dug a
hole in the ground and hid his master's money.
After a long time the master of those slaves
came and settled accounts with them. Then the
one who had received the five talents came
forward, bringing five more talents, saying,
"Master, you handed over to me five talents; see,
I have made five more talents." His master said
to him, "Well done, good and trustworthy slave;
you have been trustworthy in a few things, I
will put you in charge of many things; enter into
the joy of your master." And the one with the*

two talents also came forward, saying, "Master, you handed over to me two talents; see, I have made two more talents." His master said t o him, "Well done, good and trustworthy slave; you have been trustworthy in a few things, I will put you in charge of many things; enter into the joy of your master." Then the one who had received the one talent also came forward, saying, "Master, I knew that you were a harsh man, reaping where you did not sow, and gathering where you did not scatter seed; so I was afraid, and I went and hid your talent in the ground. Here you have what is yours." But his master replied, "You wicked and lazy slave! You knew, did you, that I reap where I do not sow, and gather where I did not scatter? Then you ought to have invested my money with the bankers, and on my return I would have received what was my own with interest. So take the talent from him, and give it to the one with the ten talents. For to all those who have, more will be given, and they will have an abundance; but from those who have nothing, even what they have will be taken away. As for this worthless slave, throw him into the outer darkness, where there will be weeping and gnashing of teeth.

Matthew 25:14-30

On Living in the Now

- ⚿ The only way we can learn to live or love is right here and now.

- ⚿ As we age, we sometimes we find ourselves living in the past—spending our time indulging in our fond memories or feeling guilty about things we did wrong or maybe just failed to do.

- ⚿ In doing so, we often miss what is happening now.

- ⚿ When we worry about the future, on the other hand, we can be overcome with infectious, fear-producing emotions. We foretell the future, imagining the worst thing that could happen.

- ⚿ When we gaze into the future with fear, there is no love.

- ⚿ We can never grow if we assume that everything will be the same tomorrow as it was yesterday.

- ⚿ James Taylor says, "The secret to happiness is enjoying the passage of time."

On Stopping to Smell the Roses

O⊸ When one task is completed, some people start another, never taking time to enjoy what they have done.

O⊸ We live in a society of immediacy which tells us that things need to be done right away, but Jesus says, "By your endurance you will gain your souls" (Luke 21:19).

O⊸ Life is a journey, not a destination. Enjoy the trip.

O⊸ Most people will be about as happy as they decide to be.

On Getting Stuck in the Past

O⊸ No one can bring back a moment gone by.

O⊸ One problem we older adults face is our natural tendency to relish past joys and relive the battles we had when we were younger.

O⊸ As we get older, we naturally tend to deal with life in certain set patterns. When new situations with their new demands disturb us, we may tend to run away from them and hold on to our old ways of doing things.

- On the surface this may seem rather harmless, but there is a danger in old ways of doing things. The danger is that we may miss the wonderful challenges and opportunities of the present moment.

- Life each day offers us opportunities to open our lives to something new and rich: new people to get to know, interesting new areas of knowledge, new feelings to understand and deal with, new ways that God is present in our lives.

- Life is what is coming, not what was. If we are absorbed in the past, we are not able to appreciate the present or prepare for the future.

On Time

- One of the major ills of old age is the fear of time.

- The encounter with time is the most stunning shock that comes to anyone. In our younger years, we are too busy to react to time; in our older years, time may become a nightmare.

- Time is our most important frontier, the place where our true freedom lies.

- The treasures of time lie open to everyone.

- Time is the process of creation.

- Time is a perpetual novelty. Every moment is a new arrival, a new bestowal.

- Just to be present in time is a blessing; just to live is holy.

- Our chief task is to sanctify time.

- All it takes to sanctify time is the acceptance of God in our lives and the appreciation of the preciousness of the present moment.

On the Present Moment

- What we have this moment is a gift—that is why it is called the present moment!

- Some older adults think of themselves as belonging to the past, but it is precisely the openness to the present that we must strive for.

- One who lives in the present moment knows that to become older does not mean to lose time but rather to gain time.

- Nostalgia has its place. However, we can become disillusioned with the present and get out of balance as a result.

- Spiritual balance can be restored by remembering Saint Augustine's words: "Do everything as though it were the most important act in the world, but also as though you were going to die the next minute and it didn't make any difference."

- We know that we need to live our best, act our best, and think our best today.

- We cannot change the mistakes of yesterday. We can make sure that our behavior today does not create more problems for the future.

- We cannot control the wind, but we can adjust our sails.

- We are in control of our perceptions, our attitudes and our responses. The power to be happy is at our fingertips, if only we choose to live in the present moment.

- No one can ruin our day without our permission.

- If we greet the day wearing a smile, confident that we are doing our best, we will discover that the day holds great promise.

☛ Success stops when we do.

☛ We carry within ourselves the image of the picture of ourselves we are creating.

☛ "This is the day that the LORD has made; let us rejoice and be glad in it" (Psalm 118:24).

Questions for Reflection or Discussion

1. Does time drag by or go too fast for you? Describe why.

2. How can the past and the present help you have a better future?

3. How are you living in the present moment? Give examples.

4. Reflect upon the fact that "now" is the only time we really have.

5. How much time do you spend each day worrying about the past and/or the future? How effective has it been for you?

Suggestions for Action

■ *Construct a daily time schedule for yourself. Decide how much time you want to spend on the past and the future. Then spend the rest of your time on living in the present.*

■ *Establish a plan to educate yourself by reading or observing something new each day. Find someone with whom you can discuss the new things you have learned.*

The Fourth Key
Accept God's Plan for You

Do not store up for yourselves treasures on earth, where moth and rust consume and where thieves break in and steal; but store up for yourselves treasures in heaven, where neither moth nor rust consumes and where thieves do not break in and steal. For where your treasure is, there your heart will be also.

Matthew 6:19-21

On the Purpose of Life

O—π Life is not the pursuit of a frantic schedule of hourly events. We can look for the deeper meaning or purpose in our life.

O—π If we keep our lives in spiritual balance, we will not get puffed up by any little triumph nor squashed by any defeat.

- It would surely be a mistake to be so busy with our work and other affairs that we give no time, thought or effort to the ultimate meaning of our lives.

- We come into this life with no worldly things, and we will leave this life without any worldly things.

- We never see a U-Haul truck following a hearse on the way to a cemetery or see drawers in a casket to hold a person's possessions.

- Just as we need to think and talk about the meaning of life, so too we need to think and talk about accepting God's plan regarding our death.

On the Spirituality of Death

- We tend to forget that we are only passing through this world. Most of us act as if we were here to stay.

- We should deepen our spiritually on earth by planning for our union with God in heaven.

- If we listen to the stillness within, we will discover what to keep and what to let go.

- Francis Bacon said, "Death is a friend of ours. He who is not ready to entertain him is not at home."

- Death is not simply something that happens to us. It is as much a part of our lives as being born.

- Death is one of the most important actions of our lives.

- From the moment we are born, we should be preparing to die.

- There is an old expression, "When your ship comes in, make sure you are willing to unload it."

- Some people do everything they can to blot death from their consciousness. They seldom succeed.

- The early Christians do not seem to have suffered any great inhibitions against talking about death, even when it was not a question of martyrdom. Their tombs and inscriptions give the impression of a quite cheerful familiarity with and even a reverence for death.

- We can all profit by one another's experiences of dealing with death. Sharing can clarify our thoughts, rid us of false fears, and put our mind at ease.

o— If, by chance, death comes suddenly and unannounced, it should not find us unprepared.

o— If we have learned to die a little each day as well as to live fully, death will come as a friend. Then we will be able to say easily, "Thank you, God, for these additional years of life."

On the Next Life

o— If we were anticipating traveling to a foreign country, we would be happily thinking about new and old friends we would meet. So why not do this when we are preparing to go to heaven?

o— Fear of death may be a lack of faith in the resurrection of Jesus and his promise of eternal life.

o— We are always looking for good in this life, and we will someday experience fullness of all Good for eternity.

o— Heaven is God's special surprise for us.

Questions for Reflection or Discussion

1. What things are truly important for you to do now, knowing that the day of your death is (by definition) drawing nearer?

2. Do you fear death? If so, what do you fear about it?

3. Reflect on what is truly meaningful in your life.

4. What do you believe about life after death? What are some of the images of heaven that come to your mind?

5. Do you accept God's plan for your death? Explain.

Suggestions for Action

■ *Decide what hymns or prayers you would like to have at your funeral. Write them down and put them where your loved ones can easily retrieve them.*

■ *Share with someone your honest thoughts about what you expect to happen at the time of your death. Reflect on whether or not your beliefs are in keeping with Christian teaching.*

The Fifth Key
Share Yourself with Others

I give you a new commandment, that you love one another. Just as I have loved you, you also should love one another. By this everyone will know that you are my disciples, if you have love for one another.

John 13:34-35

On Being Aware

⚬⊸ In our older years, we sometimes need to open our eyes to what is truly in the best interest of others.

⚬⊸ You will notice that a turtle makes progress only when it sticks out its neck.

⚬⊸ When speaking with another person, we must look into his or her eyes and listen as intently as we can, not thinking of what we are going to say next. We cannot at the same time actively listen and also be planning how we are going to respond.

O—⊓ We sometimes feel we need to fill up every possible moment of silence.

O—⊓ There is an old Native American teaching: "You must stop talking to yourself."

O—⊓ We express love through attempting to understand what another person's needs might be and then actually doing something meaningful in response to those needs.

On Giving

O—⊓ We need to look for ways to give in the right way, at the right time.

O—⊓ When we give ourselves freely to others, even to people we do not know, and expect nothing in return, we obtain the highest level of connectedness that can be achieved.

O—⊓ When our generosity is "unnoticed giving," it most closely resembles God's goodness.

O—⊓ Winston Churchill said, "We make a living by what we get; we make a life by what we give."

On Connectedness

O—¬ Enjoying another's company is life enhancing from almost every perspective.

O—¬ Those of us who have cultivated some positive interest in helping our fellow human beings will suffer far less from loneliness than those whose life has been concentrated upon themselves.

O—¬ Life's precious moments do not have value unless they are shared.

O—¬ When we become disconnected from other people, we can easily become more and more self-centered and self -absorbed. Those who fall into such an emotional posture are frequently quite unaware they are doing so.

On the Example of Jesus

O—¬ Jesus has shown us the way to be available to others—not just in words but also by example.

O—¬ Jesus is the living proof that life can be happy, meaningful and fulfilling when we put others first, loving them in the same way as he loves us.

- God's presence is made visible in the love we have for others in our daily lives.

- When we love people, they experience God's love.

- When we are loved by others, we experience God's love.

- Jesus never said caring for others would be easy, but it makes all the difference in the world between a mere existence and a meaningful, joy-filled, worthwhile life.

- The invitation to love is offered to each of us. The choice is ours to make.

On the Need to Be Needed

- The need to be needed is the source of some of the deepest longings God has planted in us.

- When we feel that no one or no institution needs us any longer, we can feel useless, good for nothing. Yet each of us is always needed somewhere in some capacity.

- Even if in our old age we are no longer able physically to help others, we can always pray.

○⟍ In the end, prayer is the most needed and longest lasting help that anyone can offer.

○⟍ We need to share the Lord with others while, in turn, we enjoy the almost hidden presence of God as it is revealed in them.

○⟍ Often our fears keep us from reaching out to others who may really need us: fear of what may be asked of us, fear of having to give up something of our self, fear that someone will take advantage of us, fear of losing some of our pride, fear of our own inadequacy.

○⟍ Fear of the unknown can keep us imprisoned in our own little world, missing out completely on Jesus' promise of joy and the wonders of what we can give to others.

On Availability

○⟍ Being available to others is not just giving time, money or advice.

○⟍ Love is not saying a lot of words, completing a compulsive list of works, trying to respond to everyone's expectations. Love is developing an attitude based on looking for and bringing God's love everywhere.

- We are commanded to love one another, even strangers. If we do, we will find joy.

- Yet we live in an age when we are increasingly fearful and defensive, anxiously clinging to our property, looking at our surrounding world with suspicion, always expecting an enemy to suddenly appear, intrude and do us harm.

On Friendship

- We need to be free and open to new friendships and relationships that can be newly and fully formed and developed in our golden years.

- For us to have a best friend, we have to be one.

- We read throughout the Scriptures that we are to be hospitable to everyone: "Do not neglect to show hospitality to strangers, for by doing that some have entertained angels without knowing it" (Hebrews 13:2).

- Unfortunately, in our old age we often become reluctant to open ourselves to new people. We may prejudge another because they speak another language or have a different skin color. We assume every stranger is a potential danger.

O—ℸ We need to humbly acknowledge our own hostilities and fears, creating a free space where a stranger can enter our life and become a friend.

O—ℸ True friendship does not manipulate others or try to control them by bringing them over to our way of thinking.

O—ℸ Finding space for others in our life is not an easy task. It requires concentration, unselfish thinking, devotion and sacrifice.

O—ℸ We cannot change other people by our personal conviction, advice or persuasion, but we can encourage, comfort and console them.

O—ℸ We can offer our friendship to another with the hope that change can take place in both of us.

Questions for Reflection or Discussion

1. What prevents you from understanding the needs of other people? What could you do to become better at this?

2. Describe one thing you did this week to share yourself with another? What did you gain personally from this interaction?

3. How connected do you feel with others—your neighbors, the people at your church, your relatives? What could you do to reach out to them?

4. Give some examples from the gospels of how Jesus made himself available to others.

5. Who is the last new friend that you made? How long ago was that? What acquaintance in your life might be a likely candidate to become your friend?

Suggestions for Action

■ *Arrange to talk with a person whom you think might be lonely. Try listening as well as you can. Realize what you are getting out of the exchange.*

■ *Set a goal of trying to make one new friend in the next month. Reach out to that person, perhaps inviting him or her to dinner or for coffee. If appropriate, suggest that the two of you do something together, such as going to a movie or a church service.*

The Sixth Key
Be Aware of the Love of Others

Love is patient; love is kind; love is not envious or boastful or arrogant or rude. It does not insist on its own way; it is not irritable or resentful; it does not rejoice in wrongdoing, but rejoices in the truth. It bears all things, believes all things, hopes all things, endures all things. Love never ends.

1 Corinthians 13:4-8

On the Nature of Love

O⇥ The more we give away love, the more we get it back.

O⇥ We are enveloped in a great web of love.

O⇥ If we try, we will find love in places where we least expect it.

O⇥ Love must be totally without prejudgment.

O── If we truly love people—including defiant teenagers, ungrateful children, disabled or feeble elderly, street people, etc.—we must love them as they are.

O── We must love all that is truly human.

O── We need to realize we can be the *agents* of love, not merely its beneficiaries.

O── If our love is restricted to a few individuals and limited to conventional acts of kindness, it will be powerless before the complexity of the modern world's problems.

On God's Love

O── Just as God's love for each person has no limit in intensity, so it has no limit in variety, depth and scope.

O── Our love for each other should reflect similar qualities.

O── We grow in the concept of love as we discover new ways in which God's presence is made known to and through us.

O── We need to think about what it means to be loved—actually, genuinely and unconditionally—by the God who created the world and all things in it.

O⟶ God loves us individually with an affection that we can only imagine.

O⟶ If we do not fully experience the love of God, our earthly joy will be incomplete.

O⟶ "Who will separate us from the love of Christ? Will hardship, or distress, or persecution, or famine, or nakedness, or peril, or sword...? For I am convinced that neither death, nor life, nor angels, nor rulers, nor things present, nor things to come, nor powers, nor height, nor depth, nor anything else in all creation, will be able to separate us from the love of God in Christ Jesus our LORD" (Romans 8:35, 38-39).

On Love in Old Age

O⟶ No matter how age may rob us of strength of body and mind, it cannot rob us of our spirit and of the power to share God's love with each person we encounter.

O⟶ We need the courage to love others as God loves us.

- There is, by definition, no condition of mind or body that prevents us from practicing some form of God's love with others.

- As long as the breath of life remains in us—even if we are reduced to total helplessness—we can still love.

- Old age is the time when we need the courage to think more of other people, rather than less—to go out of ourselves, rather than to close the curtains and brood.

- In our later years, we have the opportunity to explore and the privilege of comprehending new corners of the immense dimensions of God's love.

- As we grow older, we need to look at love as we did as a child, with eyes blindfolded to the human imperfections around us.

On Accepting Love from Others

- Jesus opened himself up to the love of others: "As he sat at the table, a woman came with an alabaster jar of very costly ointment of nard, and she broke open the jar and poured the ointment on his head" (Mark 14:3).

- This woman was living in the moment and so was Jesus. She was a role model of giving, and Jesus graciously accepted her gift. Together, they completed a story of love.

- Observing love between any of its members can spur love in a whole community of people.

- Seeing love in others is pure inspiration that expands our thinking.

- Accepting love allows us to see the true nature of another person. In that revelation we also experience the love of God.

- Being loved by others puts into reality the promise of God's love.

- If we study the lives of the saints, we will see in their actions the depth of the mystery and grandeur of God's love.

Questions for Reflection or Discussion

1. Is there a particular person or group of people whose love you find difficult to accept? Why? What might you do to become more open?

2. What does it mean to you as a Christian to truly love—and be loved by—your "brothers and sisters"?

3. Is the love you share with others dependent on certain conditions that you are applying (either consciously or subconsciously)? What are those conditions?

4. As you grow older, what are the special challenges you find in giving or accepting love?

5. How can you be more appreciative of the love you receive from those with whom you live or work or volunteer?

Suggestions for Action

■ *Make a drawing of the "web of love" in which you are enveloped. Even if you do not know them personally, make sure you include all the people who care about you (for example, people in your church, police and firefighters, and so forth). Reflect on this drawing once a week and think about whether you are making the web larger or allowing it to shrink.*

■ *Send a note to a person who has shown a lot of love to you recently. Express your sincere appreciation for that love.*

The Seventh Key
Appreciate Yourself

Do not let your hearts be troubled. Believe in God, believe also in me. In my Father's house there are many dwelling places. If it were not so, would I have told you that I go to prepare a place for you? And if I go and prepare a place for you, I will come again and will take you to myself, so that where I am, there you may be also.

John 14:1-3

On Self-Esteem

○━ People with self-esteem believe deeply within themselves that they are good and lovable.

○━ Some people have lost or have never had the opportunity to discover the truth, beauty and goodness inside themselves. These people think of themselves as somehow less able, less attractive, less worthy than they are.

- They may have carried this image with them all their lives. Often it was an insensitive parent or teacher who planted that self-image without even realizing it: "Why are you so dumb?" or "Why can't you be like your brother or sister?"

- The spark that builds and restores self-confidence starts from within.

- We must be encouraged by the potential of our future—not put ourselves in the hands of those who are determined to drag us down.

- We have total power to control how we react to the criticism of others.

- We cannot really love others unconditionally when we still feel the need to prove our own self-worth.

- Self-worth is the basis of being a good neighbor.

On God's Plan for Us

- When a person has low self esteem, it is difficult—and in some cases almost impossible— for him or her to feel loved by God, accepted by God, and worthy of God's kingdom.

- As we grow older, we need to remember that nothing befalls us nor can happen that God does not know about and does not will for our greater good.

- Added to that is the assurance that God, whose providence guides our lives, is not a tyrant who delights in seeing us suffer. God loves us and knows what is best for us.

- God is likewise infinitely powerful and always does what is best for us, even though with our limited minds we may not see or understand how this can be true.

- If we have done our best, we can let God take care of the rest.

- When we admit we are capable of being holy, we will be truly open to God's transforming power.

On Lifelong Growth and Learning

- Some people have made up their mind that they have learned all they need to learn.

- When we think we know all the answers, we really don't know the questions. Growing and learning are lifelong pursuits.

- As we grow older, faith is the primary support needed for courage and acceptance.

- Every time life asks us to give up a desire, change our direction, or redefine our goals, and every time we lose a friend, break a relationship, or start a new plan, we are invited to widen our perspective and touch the deepest currents of hope.

- Every time we are jolted by life, we are faced with the need to make new choices.

- To have a peaceful mind, we need to dwell on the good and let go of the negative aspects of life.

On Comparing Ourselves to Others

- We were all created by God, and God did a great job on each one of us!

- We need not be overcome or upset by another person's talents. God has given each of us different gifts.

- The way we look at ourselves and feel about ourselves will determine our relationships with other people and with God.

○━ Some people look at themselves and others as if they were looking at amusement park mirrors that distort the true image.

○━ We need to develop the picture of ourselves and others from the mirror God holds, not from the false reflections that may have come out of our past.

○━ God loves all of us so deeply that we are honored by being called children of God: "See what love the Father has given us, that we should be called children of God; and that is what we are" (1 John 3:1).

○━ God has declared our value: We are each someone whom God values so highly as to give the life of his own dear Son Jesus for our redemption (see Romans 5:7-8, 11).

On False Humility

○━ The idea that belittling ourselves is pleasing to God—that false humility is necessary for our sanctification and holiness—runs counter to the very basic teachings of Christian theology.

- The great commandment is that we love God with all our being. The second commandment is an extension of the first—that we love our neighbor *as we love ourselves.*

- A proper realization of our self-worth, then, is the foundation of Christian love of others.

- The person who has proper self-esteem is healthier in every way than the person with low self-esteem.

- We often think of humility as a kind of bowed-head self-hatred. This is a perversion of humility and a misinterpretation of the most beautiful of God's gifts.

- To be truly humble is to recognize that God has loved us from before we were born and loves us still.

- To be truly humble is to throw off the shackles of our perfectionism.

Questions for Reflection or Discussion

1. Make a list of all the things you like about yourself.

2. How do you react when someone compliments you? Can you acknowledge their expression of affirmation or do you have to denigrate yourself in some way? Why?

3. What are you presently doing to expand your self-esteem? How does the knowledge that you are a child of God help?

4. Give some examples of how you compare yourself with others. Is this helpful or counterproductive? Why?

5. In what ways are you still growing and learning in your older years? What new methods could you utilize?

The Eighth Key
Pardon Yourself and Others

Be angry but do not sin; do not let the sun go down on your anger, and do not make room for the devil.... Put away from you all bitterness and wrath and anger and wrangling and slander, together with all malice, and be kind to one another, tenderhearted, forgiving one another, as God in Christ has forgiven you.

Ephesians 4:26-27, 31-32

On Resentment

o━╖ The thieves that steal our good health in old age include blame, judgment, criticism, brooding and anger.

o━╖ These germs spread poison within us and prevent our vital, joy-filled garden from growing.

O— People who can forgive live much more gracious, integrated and satisfied lives than those who harbor resentments.

O— Often we carry for years an injustice long forgotten by everyone but ourselves. It is a cancer within us—a roadblock to God's mercy.

O— Stubborn people do not grow.

On Anger

O— When we allow ourselves to be angered by the actions of others, we have decided—consciously or unconsciously—to allow them to control us.

O— If we are angry, our ability to do what should be done is grossly diminished.

O— Anger can and will consume us if we allow it to.

O— When we learn to accept events that we can do nothing about and appropriately address issues that we can do something about, we can stop spinning our wheels with unproductive anger and start using our anger constructively.

O— We must let it go if we are to grow.

On Guilt

O⟶ Another form of self-punishment is guilt.

O⟶ Guilt comes in many guises. There can be genuine guilt or distorted guilt.

O⟶ Genuine guilt is an alarm that warns us of a wound we have inflicted.

O⟶ Genuine guilt leads us to reestablish friendship with those we have hurt and to establish stronger bonds with them.

O⟶ Genuine guilt also motivates us to make changes in our lives.

O⟶ Distorted or false guilt distracts us from what we can do to make things better.

O⟶ Distorted guilt can sap our life of pleasure and enjoyment.

O⟶ Distorted guilt seldom permits us to be grateful for what we have accomplished or to laugh at our foibles.

O⟶ When its sting turns inward, guilt becomes a curse.

O⟶ Feeling unworthy, ashamed, humiliated or disgraced can derail us and divert our energy into punishing ourselves.

On Compulsiveness

O—⚷ To overcome distorted guilt, we may turn to compulsiveness—filling our days with work, new duties and even good works. We become compulsive helpers, who respond to every need of every person.

O—⚷ A compulsively guilty person is constantly apologizing.

O—⚷ Some people try to take on the responsibilities of the world.

O—⚷ We alone, with our finite resources, are not solely responsible for the world.

O—⚷ There are limits to our strengths and gifts. We cannot do everything or remedy all the wrong, injury, harm or corruption in the world.

O—⚷ Even as we take on new responsibilities, we must let go of dreams that no longer fit our life.

O—⚷ One person who knew the destructiveness of compulsive guilt was Saint Augustine. At the moment of Augustine's conversion, he said: "I let up on myself a little." This is when and where his healing began.

On Forgiveness

⚷ Jesus embraced sinners and did everything he could to ease the painful feeling of guilt.

⚷ In the story of a woman caught in adultery, a crowd hungry for vengeance and public humiliation surrounds the accused woman. They press Jesus to condemn her as the law demands, but he seems strangely uninterested in their self-righteous fervor and questions their credentials for rendering judgment: "Let anyone among you who is without sin be the first to throw a stone at her" (John 8:7).

⚷ Confused and disappointed, her accusers drift away. Jesus does not condemn her; instead, he urges her to avoid her self-destructive behavior and sends her on her way.

⚷ As we mature, let us never cease to realize that our God is always there to forgive us.

⚷ To forgive is to set the prisoner free. Only then do we discover that we were the true prisoner.

⚷ The best way to get even is to forgive.

- Forgiveness is not an admission that we were wrong; forgiveness acknowledges hurt has occurred and lets it go.

- Would we rather be right or happy?

- Forgiveness of others comes only when we can release our own heart.

- Giving in can be empowering.

- If we have hurt others, we need to reach out and make amends whenever possible—even if the person has passed on.

Questions for Reflection or Discussion

1. What resentments are you harboring right now? What would it take for you to let them go?

2. Recall a time that genuine guilt motivated you to make a change in your life. How was the guilt a positive thing?

3. How do you deal with anger? Do you explode? Suppress it? Are you "passive-aggressive"? What are some healthy ways that you deal with anger?

4. Is there someone in your life toward whom you harbor unresolved feelings of anger or resentment (for example, loved ones who have hurt you, family who never call, friends who never stop by)? If so, how might you reach out and forgive that person?

5. Consider how you turn guilt against yourself and how this affects your productivity. Are there ways that you turn your guilt into compulsive activity? Describe them.

Suggestions for Action

■ *The next time you are angry or resentful, find a Scripture passage that describes how God forgives. Then try to apply it in your own life.*

■ *Think of one thing you feel guilty about. Decide if it is "good guilt" or "bad guilt." If it is genuine guilt, vow to change your behavior and then forgive yourself. If it is distorted guilt, let go of it.*

The Ninth Key
Accept Change

What I am saying, brothers and sisters, is this: flesh and blood cannot inherit the kingdom of God, nor does the perishable inherit the imperishable. Listen, I will tell you a mystery! We will not all die, but we will all be changed, in a moment, in the twinkling of an eye, at the last trumpet.

1 Corinthians 15:50-52

On Letting Go and Letting God

O━ We want to be in control of our lives, yet it is the very act of letting go that frees us.

O━ Letting go allows us to see how "God writes straight with crooked lines."

O━ If we remain open to the mysterious ways God works in our lives, we will receive blessings we would never have expected.

- Seeing things from God's vantage point makes it easier for us to look beyond the momentary roadblock and see "the big picture."

- The more we let go, the more we are able to make sense out of the nonsense of our lives.

- "Life is a mystery" because we are often not able to understand why things happen in our lives. We need to see with the eyes of faith and adjust ourselves to a universe ruled by God's infinite wisdom and love.

- We should work today to give up our old ways. These words sound easy, but there is nothing easy about letting go and letting God take over.

On Accepting Our Limitations

- We must meet head-on the challenges of aging if we are to accept them, although often our character is too set in its ways to accept them graciously.

- As we grow older, things are gradually taken from us.

- There is a basic lessening of energies.

- Vision and hearing begin to deteriorate.

⚬━ Health fails as we encounter various illnesses and pains.

⚬━ Control over our bodies can be lost. Hands may become clumsy and feet unsteady.

⚬━ There may be a loss of mental powers and memory.

⚬━ We are no longer able to control situations the way we did when we were younger.

⚬━ The meaningful work we did when were young may no longer be possible for us.

⚬━ We need to offer up all this irritation or unpleasantness, weariness or pain.

⚬━ Despite our limitations, we can rekindle our faith, redefine our values, and contemplate the nature of our legacy to family, congregation and community—doing things that were not possible during our younger years because of a lack of time.

On Spiritual Loss...and Gain

⚬━ We may experience certain spiritual losses as we grow older.

O— The zeal to do things for others may occasionally vanish.

O— The patience that was once a hallmark of our personality may become less easy to exhibit because physical pain is making us irritable.

O— Even our prayer life—which was once so vital for us—may not move us as quickly or as deeply. We may still read the Sacred Scriptures or pray our devotional prayers, but we may do so with a curious lack of interest or emotion.

O— Even the basic joy we have always had in being alive may diminish.

O— We want to join with the psalmist who asks God to renew his youth "like the eagle's" (Psalm 103:5).

O— We need to realize that God is loving us, even as our physical and spiritual gifts are taken away.

O— We need to be able to say "yes" to God, even as these gifts are taken away.

O— The losses of old age are also the opportunity for a new type of prayer—a prayer of offering up, a prayer of letting go.

On Acceptance

○━ When we lose our health, our response can be, "I love you and trust in you, my God."

○━ When we lose our energy, our response can be, " I love you and trust in you, my God."

○━ When we lose our meaningful work, our response can be, "I love you and trust in you, my God."

○━ "The LORD gave, and the LORD has taken away; blessed be the name of the LORD" (Job 1:21).

○━ As we receive the crosses that accompany older age, it is an opportunity to learn how to accept as well as how to give.

○━ We need to accept kindness, patience and help from others.

○━ We need to resist the conviction that it is always better to give than to receive.

○━ Even Jesus was a receiver. We see in Sacred Scripture that Mary and Martha served Jesus. Simon of Cyrene helped him carry the cross. All during his ministry, people opened their homes to Jesus and the disciples.

O—π When we are open to receive, we give other people the opportunity to be kind, patient and generous.

O—π They are able to grow and become more mature and holy by meeting our need for their help.

O—π Through our "decrease," others are given the opportunity to "increase."

O—π God is drawing good from our "weakness" of needing others' help.

Questions for Reflection or Discussion

1. In what ways have you accepted that you cannot function in mind and in body exactly as you did in the past? In what ways are you still fighting it?

2. What are the benefits of being where you are now in life?

3. As we get older, we are the same as we always were—only more so! Name five positive characteristics you have developed over the years. How do you use them to serve others?

4. In what ways is it easy for you to trust God? In what ways is it difficult?

5. What are your true feelings when someone tries to assist you in your daily physical and/or mental functions? Why is it sometimes difficult for you to accept their help?

Suggestions for Action

■ *Write a brief personal prayer that you can say whenever you experience anxiety, anger or resentment over growing old. Put the prayer where you can find it easily and say it whenever these feelings occur.*

■ *Find an agency, church group or activity that can help you accept and deal with your physical, mental or spiritual losses in sensitive and productive ways. Participate in a spirit of acceptance and gratitude.*

The Tenth Key
Embrace Suffering

Very truly, I tell you, you will weep and mourn, but the world will rejoice; you will have pain, but your pain will turn into joy. When a woman is in labor, she has pain, because her hour has come. But when her child is born, she no longer remembers the anguish because of the joy of having brought a human being into the world. So you have pain now; but I will see you again, and your hearts will rejoice, and no one will take your joy from you.

John 16:20-22

On the Mystery of Suffering

O⟶ We know that suffering is a mystery, yet Christ gave profound meaning to human suffering.

- Out of his suffering and death came the salvation of us all.

- When we unite our pain to the suffering of Jesus, we share deeply in his life.

- Our suffering then is transformed from something personal and crippling to something universal and liberating.

- Speaking of the church, Saint Paul reminds us, "If one member suffers, all suffer together with it" (1 Corinthians 12:26).

- In his book *The Gift of Peace,* the late Cardinal Joseph Bernardin wrote, "It is in letting go, in entering into complete union with the Lord, in letting God take over, that we discover our true selves. It is in the act of abandonment that we experience redemption, that we find life, peace and joy in the midst of physical, emotional and spiritual suffering."

- We need to look on the positive side of suffering.

- It is within our power to rejoice, even when we are in pain.

- Joy in the midst of suffering is not something we feel with our emotions, yet it is a deep reality.

O— The joy comes from knowing that God is with us in the midst of the most trying circumstances, that God understands and shares our pain totally—as no human being ever could.

O— Let us pray that the Holy Spirit will continue to teach us how to carry our crosses according to the will of God, who loves us all and will carry each cross with us.

On the Passion and Death of Jesus

O— Many famous works of art depict the agony of Jesus in the garden of Gethsemane. The gravity of his decision to embrace his suffering has captured the imagination of humankind throughout the centuries.

O— Because Jesus was truly human, his passion and death were certainly painful for him.

O— Jesus prayed with such great intensity that his sweat became like drops of blood falling to the ground. He prayed, "My Father, if it is possible, let this cup pass from me; yet not what I want but what you want" (Matthew 26:39).

- ⦰ We need to picture the humiliation of the arrest, the blows with the whip, the unjust sentence, the crowning with thorns, the mocking, the carrying of the cross, the crucifixion.

- ⦰ Jesus showed us how to face the agony of suffering and death.

- ⦰ Through his suffering, he taught all of us about fidelity to God.

- ⦰ His dying on the cross was the ultimate act of love. As he stretched his arms and nails were driven through his hands, Jesus was accepting our sins, burdens, troubles and despair.

- ⦰ Love is why Jesus was born on this planet Earth. He taught us that God can no more stop loving us than the sun can stop shining.

- ⦰ When we feel the hammers of our life beating on our heads, we know that Jesus is with us, taking the blows.

- ⦰ Every tear we shed becomes Jesus' tear.

- ⦰ Jesus may not wipe the tears away, but he makes our tears his.

- ⦰ Jesus shows us how to use our brokenness as nourishment for those we love. Our very failures help heal other people's lives.

- All our sufferings can be transformed into part of Jesus' work of salvation.

On Embracing Pain

- We have many lessons to be learned in life, and often these lessons are punctuated by stabs of pain.

- Just as an owner of a vineyard prunes branches, so God prunes us. Unless a grapevine is pruned regularly, it will not bear large sweet grapes. As we are pruned, the crosses we are asked to bear become different, but they also become more meaningful for us.

- Everyone fears pain. Trying to avoid pain is natural, but fighting against pain ultimately creates more pain.

- Medically, pain can be managed and minimized. Spiritually, it can be embraced as a way to grow. We can enter into it and accept it.

- Our suffering makes it possible to understand another's pain. We are able to be healers to one another because we have shared the experience of pain.

O— Pain can stretch us and push us to grow as we discover new levels within ourselves.

O— Elizabeth Kubler-Ross said, "People are like stained-glass windows. They sparkle and shine when the sun is out, but when darkness sets in, their true beauty is revealed only if there is a light from within."

Questions for Reflection or Discussion

1. What do you admire most about the way Jesus approached his passion and death? What would you like to emulate about him?

2. How does your suffering share in Christ's redemptive work? That is, how does it help to make the world a better place or help others come to know the true nature of God?

3. List three "good" things that have come from the pain you have endured.

4. What other people do you know who are suffering? How are they handling it? Is there anything you could do to help?

5. How do you react when an unexpected sorrow or cross comes your way? How would you like to react?

Suggestions for Action

- *Take a caregiver to lunch! Ask someone who is caring for you or for someone you know to join you for lunch. Instead of talking about your pain and suffering, ask the caregiver to talk about how he or she is doing.*

- *Research the methods of pain management available today. Try one that you never heard of or have never tried before and see what happens.*

The Eleventh Key
Find Humor in Life

Jesus entered Jericho and was passing through it. A man was there named Zacchaeus; he was a chief tax collector and was rich. He was trying to see who Jesus was, but on account of the crowd he could not, because he was short of stature. So he ran ahead and climbed a sycamore tree to see him, because he was going to pass that way. When Jesus came to the place, he looked up and said to him, "Zacchaeus, hurry and come down; for I must stay at your house today." So he hurried down and was happy to welcome him.

Luke 19:1-6

On Humor

⊶ Humor is a free commodity and has no harmful side effects.

101

O—¬ The more people create humor, the more satisfied they are with life.

O—¬ Humor is a coping mechanism that allows the body to use its own natural healing resources and may decrease the need for other conventional treatment.

O—¬ Freud was one of the first to point out that humor may have a positive influence on mental health. He argued that jokes are a means of reducing stress.

O—¬ Humor and laughter have an impact on nearly all major human physiological systems.

O—¬ Laughter is good exercise. The impact on the heart of twenty seconds of hearty laughing is comparable to three minutes of hard rowing.

O—¬ Erma Bombeck said, "Laughter is inner jogging."

O—¬ According to some researchers, laughter enhances the body's immune system and reduces stress by modifying neuroendocrine hormones that are associated with stress.

O—¬ Research in psychology indicates that humor may reduce stress as well as relieve depression.

○━ Studies show that humor has a positive effect on most of the body's major systems, including the cardiovascular, skeletal-muscular and immune systems.

○━ With laughter, skeletal muscles are activated. The activity may be mild or extreme, depending on the intensity of the humor response. Face, scalp, neck, shoulders, thoracic and abdominal muscles as well as those in the arms and legs may become involved.

○━ Humor has also been shown to reduce anxiety and increase morale. It mediates the relationship between stress and mood disturbance.

○━ In other words, we all know that laughter is good for us.

○━ We cannot really laugh without feeling happy.

On Jesus' Sense of Humor

○━ The question often asked is: "Did Jesus laugh?" The answer is: "Of course Jesus laughed."

○━ Jesus was a real man who enjoyed life fully. He must have been the happiest person who ever lived. He probably danced at the wedding feast of Cana, played and laughed with children and with friends, told a bad joke or two.

○⊸ Jesus could never have really lived without laughing, and he certainly would not have been an attractive character if he had lacked a sense of humor.

○⊸ To find the real personality of Jesus, we need to approach the passages of Sacred Scripture using the method suggested by Saint Ignatius of Loyola. He encourages us to pray by placing ourselves in a biblical scene and using our imaginations to supply the details that scripture does not record.

○⊸ Let us try to picture how Jesus cheered the vigorous young men who threw aside their fishing nets and family responsibilities to follow him. Imagine how he must have smiled as he told his plain parables of faith, hope and love to the large crowds that followed him everywhere. Picture him laughing as he and his disciples walked along the dusty, dry roads and hills in Judea or sailed their fishing boats across the Sea of Galilee.

○⊸ Jesus probably learned to laugh and smile in the arms of his mother. Mary held her tiny baby, cuddling him as he gurgled and laughed back at her. As he grew older, perhaps he laughed as he played games with his father, Joseph. Jesus learned natural, pure, joyful laughter from his parents, just as most of us did.

O⇌ The humor of Jesus has been difficult to detect because we do not hear Jesus' words as they might have sounded to his first audiences. Jesus' humor apparently was not ostentatious but subtle. To recognize and accept the fact that Jesus laughed may require rethinking traditional ideas of our Lord and Savior.

O⇌ We were not present, for example, when Jesus went through the city of Jericho and was stalked by a very rich publican, a man by the name of Zacchaeus, the chief tax collector. How Jesus must have laughed when he called the man down from his sycamore tree and told him he would stay at *his* house that night!

O⇌ Jesus asked why we so easily see the speck in our neighbor's eye and fail to notice the log in our own (see Matthew 7:3; Luke 6:41). The thought of a log sticking out of our eye socket while we carefully inspect someone else's eye for a tiny speck is preposterous.

- Jesus accused the Pharisees of straining gnats and swallowing camels (see Matthew 23:24).

- Jesus uses the ludicrous image of a camel again in the saying: "It is easier for a camel to go through the eye of a needle than for someone who is rich to enter the kingdom of God" (Mark 10:25).

- Jesus probably laughed when the companions of the paralytic removed sections from the roof of the house where Jesus was staying and let their friend down through the hole (see Mark 2:1-12).

- Jesus may have laughed when Martha was so upset because her sister Mary was doing nothing to help her. We can just imagine Jesus lightly handling Martha's being "worried and distracted by many things" (Luke 10:41).

- There is an old saying: "If you want to make God laugh, tell him what your plans are." Jesus must have felt that way most of the time.

On Humor and Aging

○━ Humor may indirectly and positively affect aging by increasing our perception of our control over our own environment. In other words, we "get" the joke.

○━ Humor enables the release of internal tension and provides us a mechanism for coping with our misfortunes, ailments and anxieties.

○━ Humor is a way of looking at aging from a different point of view, lightening up its crisis episodes, and providing us with increased insight and objectivity.

○━ By focusing on the comical elements of the aging process, humor allows us to defuse the anger and/or frustration associated with growing old.

○━ Whether planned or not, laughter takes our mind off our troubles. It diverts our attention and gives us a breather when things are getting too difficult.

○━ Humor keeps us occupied for a time while our wounds are healed.

○━ At times we get so caught up in the melodrama of life that we forget what absurd creatures we really are.

O— Laughter can counter a depressed mood while reviving our sense of self-worth. The gift of humor is life-giving and invigorating.

O— If we take ourselves too seriously, we forget that ultimately everything we do is for God.

Questions for Reflection or Discussion

1. How does a good laugh make you feel? Give a recent example.

2. Have you tried to use humor to defuse or partially defuse a tense and/or angry situation? What was the result?

3. Are you able to laugh at your own foibles and mistakes? What happens when you do?

4. Do you think Jesus had a sense of humor? Why? What do you think he might have been like?

5. Do you know someone who is able to see the humor in most things? How do you feel when you are with that person?

Suggestions for Action

- *Buy a book of jokes or cartoons. Read one or two every day. If you find one you really like, share it with a friend or relative, even if you have to call the person up just to tell them the joke.*

- *Take a famous scene from the Scriptures and imagine that everyone involved was joking around, laughing and having a good time. Write down how you think the dialogue might have gone.*

The Twelfth Key
Validate Your Feelings

May the God of hope fill you with all joy and peace in believing, so that you may abound in hope by the power of the Holy Spirit. I myself feel confident about you, my brothers and sisters, that you yourselves are full of goodness, filled with all knowledge, and able to instruct one another.

Romans 15:13-14

On Recognizing Our Feelings

- Many of us, for whatever reason, never had our feelings validated while growing up.

- There is a lot of anger, depression and anxiety in our modern culture that is manifested in many of us. We need to realize that these feelings exist and try to accept them as they are so we can better work with them.

- Some feelings are good and some feelings are bad, with many feelings being somewhere in between the good and the bad.

- Sometimes we are very much aware of our true feelings—but oftentimes we are not.

- At times, our feelings seem very apparent to ourselves and to others, but in reality they are just a cover for deeper, more distressing feelings.

- We need to try to allow ourselves to recognize our feelings, so we can increase our understanding of what is going on within us.

- If we do recognize and accept our own feelings, we should be able to better relate to others in a more positive and Christian manner.

On Dealing with Our Feelings

- It is important to acknowledge our feelings, own them, and find appropriate ways to deal with them.

- Some experts say that we are controlled by our feelings. For example, if we experienced rejection, betrayal or abandonment in our formative years, the associated pain may have been so great that we block the associated feelings of anger, fear and shame from our conscious minds.

O—π Sometimes we may try to compensate for this by being a people pleaser, never being able to say no to anyone.

O—π Or we may be compulsive in a variety of ways—becoming a workaholic, a compulsive buyer, addicted to food or dependent on alcohol or drugs, for example.

O—π Such attempts to disguise our feelings can easily get out of control, because we then are not able to come to terms with our emotions and let go of our underlying distress.

O—π We must try to recognize and deal with such feelings by either resolving them or accepting them—and then letting go of them.

O—π Many thoughts that we place in our minds are evaluations and judgments about different things, like relationships and functional ability. These all have associated feelings.

O—π Some feelings can refresh us, inspire our mind, and renew our spirit, while others can diminish our heart through discouragement and disappointment.

O— We are not trapped into feeling any particular way. We can choose which kind of feelings we allow to linger.

On Not Being Trapped

O— When we become aware of our feelings, we are better able to fully participate in all that is happening around us.

O— We need to try to be honest about our feelings without dwelling on negative feelings.

O— When we suppress or try to ignore our feelings, we can send them into our joints, our stomachs and our hearts. If we do this over and over again, we can make our bodies and minds sick.

O— Another thing we sometimes do with feelings is to "kick the dog." That is, we take out our frustration on someone or something other than that which is truly bothering us. This may briefly release our tension, but it does not deal with the real problem.

O— Many suggest that we deal with our feelings through a five-step method: 1) name them, 2) claim them, 3) tame them, 4) aim them, and 5) exclaim them.

On the Blessings of Feelings

O⇥ Society does not honor feelings like fear, sadness and anxiety as readily as it honors love, compassion and gentleness.

O⇥ We do not have to dwell on our own or another's negative feelings, but we must allow them to be expressed.

O⇥ We elderly all have "down days" when we wish we were stronger. At the same time, we should appreciate and enjoy the powers we still have.

O⇥ We need to acknowledge the personal power we have over our feelings.

O⇥ As we recognize this power, we can feel pleasantly energized and proud of ourselves when we anticipate and head off a potentially stressful or threatening situation.

O⇥ We need to be absorbed in the special blessing of sensitivity from God, who does forgive us our feelings, no matter what they might be.

O⇥ Saint Paul summed it all up: "Neither death, nor life, nor angels, nor rulers, nor things present, nor things to come, nor powers, nor height, nor depth, nor anything else in all creation, will be able to separate us from the love of God in Christ Jesus our LORD" (Romans 8:38-39).

Questions for Reflection or Discussion

1. Can you identify your negative feelings when they arise? Do you acknowledge and express them? What do you do to control them?

2. How does your body respond to negative feelings?

3. How do your feelings about yourself impact your relationships with others? Give examples.

4. How can you use your relationship with God to improve the way you feel about life in general?

5. Do you find some feelings more difficult to accept or express than others? Which ones? Why are they more difficult?

Suggestions for Action

■ *Find songs that reflect various feelings that you have. Then whenever you have a particular feeling, sing or play the appropriate song. Think about what it is that evokes the feeling in you—the words, the music, the way it is sung, or just some memory it evokes.*

■ *Begin a "Feelings Journal." Each day, write about the one or two feelings (positive or negative) that you are dealing with most strongly. At the end of each month, look back in the journal and see how your feelings have changed. At the end of the year, you might want to share the journal with a close friend or a counselor.*

Afterword

I will give you the keys of the kingdom of heaven.

Matthew 16:19

It is my hope that these twelve keys will help you enjoy holier, happier golden years. People who have discovered or rediscovered the positive aspects of their own aging have a unique opportunity to share the deepest meaning of life with every person with whom they come in contact. Every human being has only one life cycle to live, but understanding and trying to improve the aging process can complete the plan God has made for each of us.

As Jesus hung on the cross on Calvary, he said: "It is finished" (John 19:30). For those of us reaching our older years, it is our calling or task to complete the work of Jesus in our lives. We do this by being living examples of love, forgiveness, patience, generosity, self-denial and virtue. We elderly can truly work miracles in today's world. If we all open our eyes and our ears, we will quickly discover that the world is really in need of mature role models. We can and should be those role models.

As the years go on, I hope that you will periodically return to the various keys in this book and realize that we all can uncover a new spirit—a new inner being—with which to end our years on earth. If we do, we will be surprised by the strength of our faith, hope and love of God and our fellow human beings.

Saint Paul spoke of the need to become increasingly aware of the surprising things emerging within us: "So we do not lose heart. Even though our outer nature is wasting away, our inner self is being renewed day by day" (2 Corinthians 4:16).

I wrote this book to remind you—and myself—of the peace that should be ours in the remaining years of our lives. I hope that each of you will find the courage and confidence to live your life to its fullest potential in preparation for our being united with God in eternity.

It is my hope that the twelve keys will help you realize that God continues to touch us in the midst of our struggles with aging. With new hope and confidence, let us end by listening once again to the words of the Apostle Paul: "For the grace of God has appeared, bringing salvation to all, training us to renounce impiety and worldly passions, and in the present age to live lives that are self-controlled, upright, and godly, while we wait for the blessed hope and the manifestation of the glory of our great God and Savior, Jesus Christ. He it is who gave himself for us that he might redeem us from all iniquity and purify for himself a people of his own who are zealous for good deeds" (Titus 2:11-14).

God bless you.

Acknowledgments

I want to thank my bishop, the Most Reverend Donald W. Trautman, for his support in my writing and my work with older adults.

In June of 1999, Bishop Trautman asked me to consider an assignment as the chaplain of the Women's Pennsylvania State Correctional Institute in Cambridge Springs, Pennsylvania. There I work closely with the women who live inside the fences of a state medium security prison. Many of these inmates are there because of some addiction, and I have learned a great deal about the value of the various twelve-step programs for rehabilitation. This is what gave me the inspiration for the twelve keys to holier, happier golden years.

I sent copies of early drafts of this book to a diverse group of people who are very competent but work in unrelated fields. My thanks to Robert and Martha D. Becker, Jonathan Coe, Charles T. Dabkowski, John and Sil Danowski, Sister Mary Louis Eichenlaub, O.S.B., Deacon Martin P. Eisert, John L. Harrington, M.D., Yoland Jeselnick, Judith Ann Klingman, Bishop A. James Quinn, Rev. Jerome S. Simmons, Arlen Twerdok, Betsy Jane Wiest and Eileen Zinchiak. It is with total gratitude that I acknowledge the time and talent they shared in the restructuring and expansion of the ideas. Each of them has great concern for the needs of older adults, and this concern has motivated them to give many hours to help make this book a reality.

Finally, may I thank my friend, Archbishop Rembert Weakland, for the thoughtful Foreword to the book. I wish him well as he retires from the Archdiocese of Milwaukee and begins his own process of aging gracefully.

Additional Resources from ACTA Publications

BEGINNING ANEW
Reflections for Retired People
Kevin Axe
Over 100 single-page reflections filled with practical suggestions for retirees on what to do with their newfound freedom. Keep several copies on hand to give to relatives, friends and co-workers as they retire. The perfect gift for all retirees. (112 pages, paperback, $8.95)

FOR OUR CHILDREN'S CHILDREN
Reflections on Being a Grandparent
Carole Kastigar
Brief reflections and everyday anecdotes celebrate both the responsibilities and rewards of grandparenting. Each single-page reflection ends with a thought-provoking quotation or saying that helps grandparents see the loving presence of God in their lives and in their grandchildren. Featured on The Today Show. (112 pages, paperback, $5.95)

DAILY MEDITATIONS (WITH SCRIPTURE) FOR BUSY GRANDMAS
Theresa Cotter
All grandmothers will find inspiration, wisdom, joy and food for thought in this delightful collection of daily reflections and Bible quotations. A different meditation for each day of the year guides grandmothers to reflect on the important things in their lives. (366 pages, paperback, $8.95)

COMFORT AND BE COMFORTED
Reflections for Caregivers
Pat Samples
Anyone caring for elderly, infirm, disabled or handicapped relatives will find a wealth of affirming, comforting thoughts in 100+ single-page reflections. Practical suggestions are presented alongside meditations on hope, patience, service and related topics, issues and concerns. (112 pages, paperback, $5.95)

Available from booksellers or call 800-397-2282 in the United States or Canada.